IT'S OKAY TO ANSWER YOURSELF

An INTERACTIVE Companion to Help You Thrive Through Aloneness

Dr. T. Bob

Forecast

Introduction	ix
Prologue	1
Minimal	
Category 1	7
SHELTER A	23
Moderate	
Category 2	27
SHELTER B	43
Extensive	
Category 3	47
SHELTER C	55
Extreme	
Category 4	59
SHELTER D	69
Catastrophic	
Category 5	73
Prescriptions	75
Notes	101
Epilogue	111
Bibliography	115
About the Author	117

IT'S OKAY TO ANSWER YOURSELF

Copyright © 2023 by DR. T-BOB

All rights reserved. No part of this book may be reproduced or transmitted in any form or by any means without written permission from the author.

Library Of Congress Cataloging: In Publication
ISBN: 9798988838807

Printed in the United States of America

And the Lord, He is the One who goes before you. He will be with you, He will not leave you nor forsake you; do not fear nor be dismayed.

Deuteronomy 31:8

Dedication

*This book is dedicated to
Inez Mackey Burton, My grandmother.
May you always know I am never alone.*

Introduction

People who talk to themselves are crazy, right? Wrong. During periods of loneliness, face-to-face conversations are limited. Yet, random conversations often occur in the minds of those living through unexpected "me time." This self-talk isn't always the dose of encouragement needed to elevate from loneliness to aloneness. Therefore, you must talk to yourself. But most importantly, ANSWER YOURSELF to combat those negative thoughts.

"It's Okay to Answer Yourself" utilizes hurricane analogies to engage and educate readers. Hurricanes can cause minimal or catastrophic damage. Additionally, electricity may fail to function. And in worse-case scenarios, there may be loss of life. Like hurricanes, loneliness and uncertainty can also cause minimal or catastrophic damage. Without the proper social and emotional tools, you may experience the latter. The level of damage depends on how we equip ourselves.

Introduction

"It's Okay to Answer Yourself" delivers knowledge from a place of experience and research. This companion is the insightful friend who always keeps it real, with a sprinkle of sugar on top. Each chapter is concluded with an interactive shelter experience to help you thrive through aloneness. So go ahead and enjoy your journey to wholeness!

Prologue

THE LOUD SILENCE

As a little girl, my grandmother sang hymns that echoed throughout her modest 2-bedroom apartment located in the St. Bernard Housing Development. Her voice was reflective of an opera singer who quit voice lessons early in the process, or maybe her instructor resigned due to a busted eardrum, who knows? I can recall covering my head with a pillow to mute the sound. After her closing note, there would always be warm conversation that opened with thanking an audience only she could hear. It was a tad confusing because there was no one else there other than she and I, and I was clearly not the focus of the seemingly grateful words being spoken.

After experiencing the older deacons at church communicating with God, I figured it out; she was praying. Yes, that's it! Still, there were other times I heard her talking, but the self-talk had nothing to do with God. Or did it? Some say as we get older, we turn into our parents.

Well maybe I took a few notes from my grandmother also. Those hymns she sang that annoyed me as a child began to comfort me in my season of aloneness. By verbally responding to my inner dialogue, I finally let the cat out of the bag and obliged my inner questions that warranted long-awaited acknowledgment.

Let's take it back to the beginning of time when God created Adam and it was good. He did not think it was good for Adam to be alone. So He extracted Adam's rib to create Eve with the plan for them to procreate and expand humankind. Thus, eliminating loneliness. Apparently, we were not created to walk the earth by ourselves. Whether you have chosen a solo situation or you are without companionship due to loss of loved ones, a lack of friends/social life, or unmarried, loneliness can hit with full force.

As a content and purposeful single woman, I too experience loneliness. After ending an engagement, grieving an unsuccessful marriage, and participating in unequally yoked courtships, I understand the journey of loneliness. This journey helped me process the difference between being alone and experiencing loneliness. We will explore the two shortly.

Many extroverts find it difficult to be alone because of the strong desire to interact with others on a regular basis. I'd like to think I am an extroverted introvert. As an introvert, being alone never truly bothered me and getting out once a week seemed to work well for my social needs. Still, an extensive period of being alone can take a toll on anyone. For some, coping with being alone can last a year or so. For others, any duration beyond a year may become dangerous. It all depends on the individual's level of stability, maturity, and spirituality. Let's unpack this later.

When compared to a hurricane, aloneness brews as a Category 1 and can potentially develop to a Category 5, destroying everything in its path. Anytime a hurricane forms, the public is notified. And once it reaches a Category 4, citizens are urged to evacuate all areas affected. This book will help identify the warning signs of loneliness and offer tips on when to seek shelter.

Like most people, I can feel loneliness sneaking up by changes in sleep patterns, poor eating habits, obsessing over past choices and struggling with loss and identity. When loneliness is labeled as a Category 1, many tend to treat it as a storm that will pass. We heed the warning without attempting to seek shelter. Right before our eyes, it grows from 2, to 3, to 4, to 5, and then BOOM! Destruction hits.

Oftentimes, destruction lands in the form of isolation, depression, loss of impulse regulation, alcohol and drug abuse, or suicidality. I believe it is time to seek shelter before the Category 5 hurricane hits. What about you?

Minimal

"Very dangerous winds will produce some damage. Some small trees may fall and cause mild damage to your home."

How do you define your home?

Category 1

IT'S NOT NORMAL

Let's talk about the exact moment you realize something isn't right. While sitting down for dinner after a long day of work, suddenly the fantasy of preparing a second plate for a nonexistent partner materializes. Before watching that nighttime comfort movie, the action of sliding popcorn in the microwave conjures a picture of two buttery hands instead of one. Becoming the recipient of good news and realizing there isn't anyone to immediately inform and spread the joy. Waking from a nightmare, reaching for your teddy bear or extra stuffed pillow that can't seem to provide the warm cuddle you need. Sudden illnesses that bring helplessness, and that trip to the medicine cabinet is too far. The thought, "It sure would be a treat if someone else was here," stings like salt in an opened wound. Or tragically, someone is there, but they are not worth the ink from the pen used to jot their number down.

The above stated thoughts are not negative; they are realistic and indicative of the turning point in a healthy decision-making process. Even though this line of thinking is innocent, it is important because all behavior begins with a thought. This is why it is essential to gain control over personal thoughts early in the game. Why do I call it a game? Because that's what it is, cat and mouse. Inner dialogue will make or break you. Positive dialogue leads to good behavior and negative dialogue leads to bad behavior.

With this idea in mind, let's explore the definition of lonely. According to Merriam-Webster, *lonely* is defined as being without company, cut off from others, not frequented by human beings, and/or producing a feeling of bleakness or desolation. To yearn for a conversation; to long for the sound of laughter; to ache for a baby's cry; to thirst for an endearing hug; to crave a simple touch, is the unexplainable feeling one may experience from loneliness. Sounds gloomy, right? Well, it can be. It's easy to feel hopeless when it seems as though the walls are closing in.

Human touch plays a significant role in human development and growth. Ask yourself, is it normal to exist in a world full of people and still feel alone? How do people live seemingly successful lives with friends and family, yet never realize that just maybe their aloneness is normal? But what exactly does this *normal* word imply? Merriam-Webster defines *normal* as conforming to a type, standard, or regular pattern. The operative word here is "con-

It's Okay To Answer Yourself

form." Who says you must conform to a particular standard? Who says you're supposed to be normal? Back in grade school, if a kid was a bit different from everyone else, he would be called weird. When describing a situation that is a bit out of the ordinary, it's sometimes said "It's just not normal." Humans are conditioned to believe that being different is not normal.

Aloneness is not weird. Feelings of loneliness are not abnormal. Humans exist in a world where there are highs and lows, mountains and valleys, sadness, and happiness. They simply need the tools to thrive through the lows, the valleys, and the sadness.

A Category 1 hurricane is said to cause minimal damage; "storm winds may knock down some trees and power lines and do a bit of damage to buildings" (Categories of Hurricanes [NCHH, 2023). As a native of New Orleans, Louisiana, I remember it like it was yesterday. In early August 2005, the meteorologist began to speak of a Category 1 hurricane, which they named Katrina. Locals paid little attention to this report. After all, it was only a Category 1. Therefore, there was no need to worry. We dismissively thought, "It's basically a heavy rain." New Orleans residents were accustomed to a little thunder and lightning and maybe even a bit of flooding.

Aloneness can also be categorized. But before diving into troubled waters, let's explore the difference between aloneness and loneliness: I define *loneliness* as <u>a feeling of sadness or emptiness, which can oftentimes lead to situational depression</u>. A lonely person can feel as though something is missing. There are many unhealthy behaviors that may accompany this feeling. On the other hand, I define *aloneness* as <u>simply being alone</u>. Albeit, during this alone time, <u>one is fulfilled, purposeful, and complete</u>.

Loneliness as compared to a Category 1 storm seems harmless, but may cause damage to thought processes and dating habits, or lack thereof. But for the most part, it is harmless, right? Nah, I disagree. Well, kinda sorta. There is no major damage here. It is in fact minimal. Nonetheless, when those side effects of loneliness begin to creep up, it is important to identify them. I know you're thinking "Okay, you explained the difference between the two, but I still get lonely sometimes, whether you call it aloneness or loneliness." Guess what? I know you do! And because you have a pulse, that is okay. No matter which way the ball bounces, we are all guilty of feeling a bit lonely and maybe even talking to ourselves, whether it is verbal or nonverbal. It's a lost art, I tell ya.

When New Orleanians received the news of a Category 1 hurricane, each person owned a thought. That thought was either "Oh it's nothing, just a mild storm" or "I should start preparing; it may get stronger." Notice how I used the term *own*? When a particular thought appears, it can be owned or dismissed.

How would you describe your "force of nature"?

While pondering the thought, you are already talking to yourself. For this reason, you must also answer yourself. What is a question without an answer? If you do not answer yourself, there will be a force of nature who will grant you a response. This is usually not the answer needed to move forward, only to set you back. Take notice, the mind has a way of playing tricks on us. Think of this part of the game as a race. Set a goal, a personal finish line if you will. How will you get there? In reaching your goal, choose to accept or challenge each thought and behavior that bears weight. Every game has opponents. You may have to run faster, jump higher, or think smarter. Whatever the case, you must win. It is never cool to come in second place, at least that is what society teaches.

We live in an age of social media where the number of followers one has influences their confidence and self-esteem. After viewing a friend's account, side conversations may sound something like this: "Girl, did you see Michelle's post last week? She just married the love of her life! He's a high-powered attorney and she still looks like she's 25." Or this: "Man I was on IG and I saw Mike just purchased his 50th property. That's dope!" Everywhere we turn, it seems like others are living normal lives. There goes that "normal" word again. Friends are exchanging marital vows, procreating, and gaining wealth, while you are struggling through aloneness. But here's the thing, what looks like milk and honey on the outside may be dry land on the inside. Social media is great, but it is a misleading representation of the life most people want to enjoy. Think about it, how many users post what is truthfully going on in their lives? Studies have linked Instagram to depression, body image concerns, self-esteem issues, social anxiety, and other problems. By design, the app capitalizes on users' biological drive for social belonging (American Psychological Association, 2021). Human beings seek approval wherever we can get it, and social media is an easily accessible place to start.

There is a little four-letter word that can tag alongside seeking approval. Can you guess what it may be? Drum roll..... envy. Envy can sneak up like a thief in the night. Sometimes it may seem innocent. But just like a thief, it is crafty and quiet. It can cause individuals to covet others' lifestyles. Let's dissect the word covet. According to the Life Application Study Bible, Exodus 20:17 states, *"You shall not covet your neighbor's house. You shall not covet your neighbor's wife, or his male or female servant, his ox or donkey, or anything that belongs to your neighbor."* A deeper dive finds "to covet" is to wish to have the possessions of others. It goes beyond simply admiring someone else's possessions or thinking to 'I'd like to have what you have.' Coveting includes envy—resenting the fact that others have what you don't." This is one of The Ten Commandments.

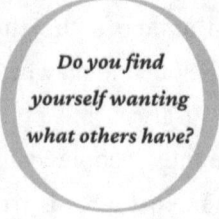
Do you find yourself wanting what others have?

Comparison is widely used to make us feel less than. Nevertheless, comparing humans and the lives we live is like comparing apples and oranges. Apples are red, do not require peeling, and provide a good source of fiber and Vitamin C. Oranges are orange, require peeling, and provide a good source of fiber and Vitamin C. Just as apples and oranges are different, but have some similarities, you may share the interests or characteristics of others, yet you are very different from the next person.

We are *fearfully and wonderfully made,* Psalm 139:14. No one else has your Deoxyribonucleic Acid (DNA). How special is that? Speaking of DNA, it is the molecule that carries genetic information for the development and functioning of an organism (National Human Genome Research Institute, NIH, 2023). The DNA from any two people is 99.9% identical. But the differing 0.1% contains variations that influence our uniqueness, which when combined with our environmental and social contexts give us our abilities, our health, and behavior.

Isn't that good news? There is clear evidence of your uniqueness. Go ahead and rejoice about that! For this reason, when the voice of comparison and envy enter your mind, remember there is only one you. Your journey will never be exactly like anyone else's. It is important to enjoy the ride, even when experiencing it alone.

Just because there's no one to hold the umbrella when it begins to rain does not negate the fact that the downpour will occur. Reaching your chosen destination requires experiencing the downpour. When the rain gets stronger, choose to run for cover or sing. Rain always starts with a drizzle. Think about it; you're driving along the street and raindrops begin to dampen the windshield, maybe enough to activate the wipers. In most circumstances, those raindrops are an indication of stronger rain. The planners may readjust their schedules, while the spontaneous are likely to wait to see what happens. I used to watch the weather report each night. Yeah, I was the type of person who needed to plan my day, specifically related to what I would wear. Because being caught off guard was not an option, I always stored a light jacket in my trunk. Preparation was key and it still is.

During a Category 1 phase of aloneness, a beginning is discovered. The beginning of a feeling, an experience, a journey, or a way of being. Look at the following phrases: prepare dinner, prepare for bed, prepare a statement. Each phrase is not led by spontaneity. To prepare dinner, one must decide what is to be cooked, gather ingredients, and proceed to bring those ingredients together to produce a finished product. Aloneness is not much different. When you fail to plan, you plan to fail.

You may be asking yourself "how can I plan for aloneness?" Sounds crazy, right? By the way, I love that you have asked yourself a question; you're catching on. Woohoo! Now go ahead and use those tools to answer yourself. Need help? Okay, I guess I can offer a bit of assistance since we are only in Category 1.

In preparing for aloneness, it is helpful to:

❖**Accept the fact that you are alone.**

Psychologist Nathaniel Branden says, "The first step toward change is awareness. The second step is acceptance." In most healing processes, acceptance is a staple step that can't be neglected. Typically, acceptance is the last stage; its placement does not deviate from its importance. Before thriving through aloneness, it is essential to acknowledge one's current state. Just as a substance abuser must accept his substance problem or a sex addict must first admit she has an unhealthy addiction to sex, a perfectly "normal" person must accept that they are alone for a time.

> *Is it difficult for you to acknowledge your feelings? How so?*

Having said that, acceptance is not giving in to dysfunction. It is saying 'This is my current situation, and now it is time to choose if I want to remain here or create a plan to break free.' Now just because I offered examples of a substance abuser or sex addict, please do not feel labeled. Aloneness is a state of being, not an addiction. Those examples are only used to provide clarity about a given reality, but do not judge too quickly. In neglecting to take the first step seriously, anyone could fall into one of those categories...just saying. Here's what else you can do.

❖Acknowledge your feelings in the moment.

Acknowledgment can sometimes be a doozy. I recall lying in bed one night wondering why I'd been single for such a long time. I asked God 'Am I being punished for something?' I thought maybe this was a consequence of an earlier action. Due to the discomfort of the situation, I hurriedly escaped the feeling.

In many cases, being alone can cause self-doubt and blame. Here again is why we must answer ourselves. To gain clarity regarding my question to God, there was no need to hurriedly escape the conversation I had in fact started. The most effective route to take would have been verbal acknowledgment of my feelings, followed by a response. It may have sound something like this, 'I am confused and I am tired of being alone. But I am not being punished.' Acknowledgment is having the insightfulness to identify those hard feelings and the courage to thrive through them. How about this?

❖**Understand that it is okay to be alone.**

The term "understand" differs from the terms accepting and acknowledging. Now that we have accepted our current state of aloneness and acknowledged those feelings, it is time to process the new emotions. I will use the terms *process* and *understand* interchangeably.

For whatever reason, you are alone. Whether you chose it or not, the outcome is consistent. That being said, the circumstances surrounding your aloneness may contribute to how you process your current state of being. If you have chosen to be alone, understanding your situation may be a bit easier. You've tried roommates; you've tried cohabitating; you've even tried moving closer to family members or moving in with family members, but it just did not work. In contrast, if you are alone due to conditions you could not control, processing may seem more challenging. Maybe you have experienced a divorce, a loss or breakup, and are constantly blaming yourself for the role you played in the real-life scenarios.

When the forecast calls for lightning, meteorologists can scientifically explain how lightning moves across the sky. Still, most do not care to hear an explanation. Those who are going to be affected by the lightning typically understand what's to come. Consequently, if they stand outside near a tree while trying to figure out the cause of the expected lightning bolt, they may get struck, which can lead to irreparable damage. No matter the circumstance surrounding your aloneness, be sure to heed the warning and protect yourself. Taking this into account, what should happen to avoid irreparable damage to your building?

❖**Decide what you want your future to look like.**

Have you ever taken a glimpse into your future? What did you see? If not, I dare you to try it. It's a fun way to imagine what life can be like. When I was in grade school, doodling was a way to totally ignore the teacher while pretending to listen. Whatever lad I'd taken an interest in would be the subject of my doodling. Matching hearts seemed to be my chosen graphic most of the time, along with our names and future offspring names enclosed within the hearts.

Being imaginative begins early. Even as an adult, who says we cannot refine the activity of doodling, which may be renamed as journaling or vision boarding. Journaling is the activity of writing down collective thoughts in a designated notebook. This is a place to share feelings, ideas, and innermost secrets. Journals are usually personal, and the owner shares at their discretion. I suggest creating a journal entry a minimum of three times per week.

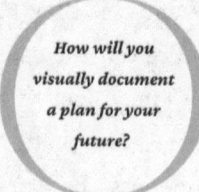

Ideally, five to six days out of a week would be most beneficial. A Vision Board is a visual display of your short and long-term goals. Typically, the creator uses cutouts from various magazines to display the future they envision for themselves. Now is the time to create your desired future. Carve out time to get it done. Here are some questions to get started:

*What type of house do you want?
*How many children do you want?
*How would you like your adult children/grandchildren to relate to you?
*What is your ideal job?
*What will retirement look like for you?
*What are the characteristics of your future spouse?

*What does your ideal marriage look like?

*What are the rules of engagement for your family unit?

*What areas of your life need healing?

*What are your financial goals?

Although psychics predict the future, you have the ability to create and speak to your future utilizing your voice and the written word. Indeed, there is power in writing and speaking aloud. *Write the vision. And make it plain on tablets, that he may run who reads it* (Habakkuk 2:2). Utilize personal foresight by writing, drawing, painting, and/or speaking. Forward thinking is key. I see you in the future and you look like royalty to me. Guess what else is helpful?

❖**Making a clear choice not to transition to extended periods of loneliness.**

After the previous steps, there must be a definitive decision made towards your sanity. As previously mentioned, we all may experience loneliness at some point in our lives. But here is where we get to the fork in the road and we must determine which way to proceed. Do we veer north or south? The storm is brewing toward the south. There is even a chance of flooding. Even though there is only minimal damage in Category 1, if the southern route is chosen, the damage can become categorically worse.

While experiencing Category 1 aloneness, it is important not to sit back quietly and ignore the hard emotions. Ignoring a feeling never makes it go away. It only delays it for a time. While moving forward with daily activities, the feeling may seem to have subsided. But when you least expect it, especially during your aloneness, it always resurfaces.

According to the National Weather Service (2022), Hurricane Katrina became a large and powerful hurricane that caused enormous destruction and significant loss of life. Katrina was responsible for 1,833 fatalities. Many lost their homes and their way of life as they knew it. Although this was difficult for many to process, there is no way to deny this life-changing fact.

Repressed emotion will deal with you if you do not deal with it, which can then lead to stress. For example, stress can affect the human musculoskeletal and respiratory system, cardiovascular, endocrine, gastrointestinal, nervous, and reproductive systems (American Psychological Association, 2023). Stay healthy people. There's a storm brewing.

An extended period of loneliness varies according to the individual. For some, one week without communicating with a loved one is typical. For others, maybe one-two days is typical. You must know yourself enough to know how long is too long to exist without hearing the voice of or being around those who genuinely care for you. If you believe there is no one who genuinely cares for you within your circle, it's time to create new bonds.

It's Okay To Answer Yourself

Notice the keywords in this directive "extended periods." This calls for motivation or what I call "get up and go". "Get up and go" generally means when you notice yourself feeling lonely and sad.... get up, get dressed, and get out of the house! Is this easier said than done? Well of course. But you can do it! No one said you had to beat your face or put on a coat and tie. Just shower, throw on clean clothes and let the sun hit your face. Vitamin D can do wonders for the spirit. In fact, a short walk has never hurt anyone. Ever silenced yourself enough to hear birds chirping? Life does not stop because you are alone. So go ahead and enjoy being outside.

SHELTER A

When was the first time you noticed an unhealthy feeling related to being alone? Please elaborate (where were you, what was the exact emotion, how did you respond).

DR. T BOB

Has your home (your body, temple, mind) incurred minimal damage? Describe your building and the damage in detail.

Moderate

"Uprooted trees can cause property damage. Roofs and siding could be damaged."

How would you describe your roof and siding?

Category 2

I'LL BE OKAY

Has there ever been a moment when you could not pinpoint exactly what was wrong, yet knew something was just not right? The sun was shining, all was well with the world, but there was still something missing. Maybe you attempted to call a loved one, though they did not pick up the phone. Perhaps you dialed your good friend, only he was not available. You turn to social media and even the Instagram models and smiley Facebook photos are not doing the trick. You discern you simply want to hear a friendly voice; the voice of someone who can hear your heart. They can hear beneath your jovial responses and exercise supernatural vision to be able to see through your smartphone.

Nevertheless, it seems as though what you need when you need it is hardly ever available. What would you have said had the person on the other end of the phone picked up? "Hey girl, I was just calling to see how you're doing" or "What's up bruh, just checking on you?" Now of course they will ask you the same question you asked of them. Are you ready for one of the most important questions of your existence? Brace yourself; HOW ARE YOU?

Seems like a straightforward interrogative sentence. However, this statement has become more of a routine amongst friends versus one that warrants a genuine response. For the most part, it is equivalent to saying "hi." I invite you to ponder the thought, 'When I ask someone this question, do I want an honest answer?' Then query yourself, 'When someone asks me this question, do I offer an honest response?' You know what to do next, answer yourself. Use your answer to determine your next steps.

Depending on where you reside, someone may ask this question as you glide up the street, as you play with your kids at the park or push your cart in the grocery store. Your typical response is usually short and sweet. Of course this person does not know you. Therefore, why should they care about your well-being? Be that as it may, how would you explain when a loved one asks, still you are not genuine with your response.

So why did I label 'How are you' as one of the most important questions of your existence? This is so because it is a part of you acknowledging your current state of mind. Yes, your current state of mind may be difficult to discuss, challenging to process, sad to relive, or even overwhelming to communicate. Thereby being easier to simply avoid those true feelings. After all, there was no real preparation for this question. I get it. But I also get that you have begun to master the role of pretending as well. I recall experiencing an uneasy feeling among friends due to a previous minor dispute, one that was never discussed or resolved. A friend in our circle invited me to a gathering, to which I responded "I believe there are some things we need to discuss before we gather. I don't think we should pretend." Let's just say my friend was not too happy with my response. And when our fellow friend got wind of my sentiment, she did not receive it favorably either.

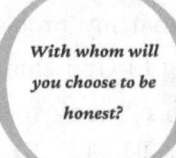
With whom will you choose to be honest?

At the time, I could not understand what was so negative about my reaction to her invitation. It appears it was my use of the word *pretend*. I chose to incorporate this term because when an individual does not feel comfortable or has underlying issues that have not been resolved, we typically pretend they do not exist, especially around others. This is something we must cease. My friends were offended because they did not want to be accused of such a crime. Had we gathered without discussing our issue, this is what we would have been guilty of in a sense. Smiling to cover up an inner frown, being nice when you really want to yell at each other, and cringing each time they turn away from you is in fact some form of pretending.

It is vital to be honest about your feelings. Only you are aware of your true sensitivities. Maybe there is someone with whom you share a close relationship. Yet, it is not wise to assume they know you better than you know yourself. When you are not okay with another human being, express your thoughts and feelings from a place of humility and respect. When you are not okay with yourself, talk to yourself. Have a conversation about the root cause, your actions following the root cause, and finally, your thought process. Do not pretend you are okay. Talk yourself through the process.

Many times, depression sets in and difficulties are handled alone. In a candid conversation with my mom regarding my viewpoint of families seeking therapy, she nonchalantly stated "I talk to God about my problems." Certainly, I am not opposed to talking to God almighty about any problem encountered on this bumpy road of life, which is marred by potholes, roadblocks, detours, stop signs, and speed bumps. Still, be reminded that God sends people to translate His message. After all, the Bible was written by men <u>divinely inspired</u> by God.

If you have a heart, most people will experience sadness or loneliness at some point in their lives. It is simply an unfortunate part of life. A part that we usually cannot control. Over the years, I recall hearing the sentiment - either you've been through a storm, you're going through a storm, or a storm is on the way. While living through the pandemic of the Coronavirus Disease, it is almost impossible to not feel moments of sadness. So many lives lost, separation of families, and the lack of human touch was a sure way to bring on some form of depression. According to the Journal of Counseling Psychology (2020), "when we isolate ourselves from others, we are at much greater risk for loneliness and reduced self-esteem. We know that isolation and uncertainty, when mixed in sufficiently large quantities, form a powerful cocktail for anxiety, depression, and suicidal ideation."

Albeit these were the exact instructions given during the height of the pandemic, to socially distance ourselves. As we often do, we found a slight way around it. Yup, you guessed it, technology. We enjoyed technology daily. There's FaceTime and various forms of video technology. Even so, there is simply something about *touch*. Place human beings together and there will surely be a handshake, a pat on the back, a high-five or a firm hug that can melt any hardened heart. Ever notice the enveloping warmth of a good, tight hug from a genuine person? Ever revel in the feeling of hand-holding with a partner? Ever simply lean on a friend's shoulder while watching a movie or having a conversation? *Touch* is a powerful feeling. It can be healing.

Many find it difficult to isolate themselves. Sometimes it simply happens because of a saddened state of mind. However, when you're being made to isolate yourself based on a "safer at home" order, it just doesn't seem right. After all, you are an adult. No one tells you when to come and go. But hey, you've got this under control. You are the master of your sea and the captain of your ship. Although your ship is starting to encounter rough waters, you pay no mind to it. The drizzle has progressed to a nice flow of rain in which you surely need an umbrella to avoid some level of dampness. If you choose not to use an umbrella for coverage, you will in fact endure the consequences. In this analogy, the consequences may not be steep. A little rain never harmed anyone, right? Of course not. Conversely, a little sadness can.

As mentioned earlier, everyone experiences a bit of sadness due to life circumstances. These feelings are inevitable. While these feelings of sadness may be unavoidable, when an extended period of sadness falls upon you and consequently affects your daily activities, you have moved past grabbing an umbrella for protection. This is why I need you to reach for it as soon as the drizzle begins.

"I'll be okay" is a great belief to verbalize if you truly believe it. On occasion, those with genuinely high confidence levels or those who rely on a higher power will express this way of thinking with no doubt. Singer and First Lady Erica Campbell tells the story of learning her husband, Pastor Warryn Campbell II, was diagnosed with cancer. While getting pampered at a day spa, she became frantic. Right before phoning her sister, the receptionist asked if she was okay. She responded "no, but I will be." Beyond the shadow of a doubt, she knew through prayer, she would be okay. With time, Erica and Pastor Campbell were in fact healed and okay.

As opposed to full-of-faith thinking, there are those who verbalize this belief as a form of denial or to shrug off their uncomfortable feelings. It is almost a way of providing a quick response to avoid further conversation. Because who knows, there may be more questions and more digging if this belief isn't assertively verbalized. The questioning party may even sense something is wrong. And we don't want that to happen, now do we?

Now let me be clear, please use wisdom and intuition when choosing to share personal information. Not everyone cares about supporting your emotional well-being. That's a different book for a different time. If this is someone you have chosen to share with, he just may provide a safe space to begin your healing process.

"What if I do not have a person I can trust in my circle?" you ask. This question does not surprise me. People are flaky and imperfect. Yes, I said it. For all I know, you have experienced someone gossiping about you, lying on you, or betraying your trust.

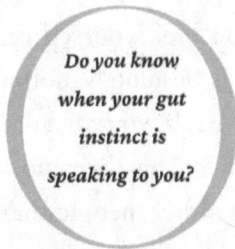
Do you know when your gut instinct is speaking to you?

Sometimes it is generally an uneasy feeling as it relates to a specific individual. It could be that being alone for such a lengthy period has caused feelings of 'not needing anyone' to become a stronger thought. Or potentially trust is something you struggle with. You struggle because no one checks in on you and a nice gesture is far from common. Without a doubt, I am not recommending you forget those things that make up your reality. But again, I am suggesting you pull from your gut to make a wise decision.

During the moderate stage of a hurricane, "storms are likely to uproot many trees, disrupt electric power over wide areas and do significant roof and siding damage." Have you answered the question at the top of this chapter... How would you describe your roof and siding? Roof and siding damage are determined on a case-by-case basis. Some examples of roof and siding damage are:

❖**Isolating yourself, even when you are not required to.**

Your friends continue to invite you out, though you always have an excuse. From needing to get work done to having to bathe your cocker spaniel, there is always something superseding a friendly invitation to have fun. When was the last time you dressed nicely for an evening away from the house?

Okay, so you don't favor hanging out in crowds. No worries. When was the last time you took yourself on a date? Yes, that's a thing and there is absolutely nothing wrong with it. If you can answer yourself, you can surely take yourself out. Do you know why this behavior is totally sane? Because there will be other people there. Imagine that. Even though you are alone, remain open to meeting and conversing with others by smiling and being friendly.

This one is a real keeper: answer your phone! Did I say that loud enough? Did they hear me in the back? Contrary to what your sometimes less than positive thoughts can lead you to believe, there is at least one person walking this earth who is concerned about your well-being. Do not shut them out due to the transgressions of others. Whilst you may not feel like entertaining what you believe to be meaningless conversation, you can always choose to communicate via text messaging. Texting is a great way to maintain a reasonable amount of distance while remaining present. So, respond to the text and answer the phone call. You never know what's on the other side of that smart gadget. Here's another one:

❖Becoming barren through busyness.

We should start by breaking down the term barren. In various instances, when this term is used, it references a female who is not able to carry or bear children. Merriam-Webster defines barren as "incapable of producing offspring, used especially of females or mating." If we dig deeper, it is also defined as "producing little or no vegetation, unproductive of results or gain, lacking interest or charm, and lacking inspiration or ideas." Busyness is described as "the state of having or being involved in many activities."

What damage has the storm caused in your life?

So how can one become barren through busyness? Due to your roof and siding having already begun to experience moderate damage, the societal norm is to find a way to cover it up. How about if you notice aesthetically unpleasing storm damage to your actual house? Because of the concern of others' opinions, your thoughts begin to race trying to determine how to perfect your roof and siding. Let's see, it is possible that three coats of paint will do the trick. It's not about the paint but about the amount of work it will take to apply.

Let's make this a bit more practical. In the midst of the storm, you become involved in a boatload of activities and tasks that cause an impassive reaction to your aesthetically unpleasing home. You have been so busy all day and now exhaustion sets in. In fact, the damage has been there so long it doesn't even bother you anymore. You know the home is damaged, but it has become normal. If someone asks about it, you simply begin to brag about all the other things you have going on. Consequently, not having time to repair the root problem.

What is your root problem? What damage has the storm caused in your life? It is important to identify your root problem because it can lead to the reason for your potential barrenness. Maybe your storm is divorce, singleness, abandonment, guilt, physical or emotional abuse, unforgiveness, addiction, or self-doubt. No matter the storm, it is connected to the root problem.

ROOT PROBLEM → STORM
→ BUSYNESS → BARRENNESS

Now this does not have to become the flow chart of

your life. After identifying the root problem and the storm, this is where opening your mouth and talking to yourself is helpful. Ask yourself:

What are my next steps?

1. Who can I talk to about my storm?
2. Should I speak with a mental health professional?
3. What can possibly happen if I choose to ignore the root problem?

❖Ever consider becoming a "loner?"

A loner is a person who has no interest in being around other people. Becoming a loner can totally be a side effect of a moderate storm. Earlier, I touched a bit on potential trust issues, along with the imperfection of humans. Please allow me to elaborate a bit more. Disappointment after disappointment can be a bit draining. How many apologies can one accept? Or how can one process that an apology will never happen?

What do you say we begin with those we love most? Sounds good? Okay. Those we love most possess the power to penetrate our heart. I don't know about you. But there have been many times when family members have caused me to step a little out of character. Who am I kidding? A lot outside of character. After several dysfunctional occurrences, a little voice in my head said, "Just stay away. It's so much better when you don't come around as often." I responded to myself, "Yup, I think I'll do that." Does this sound familiar? It is easier to avoid conflict when you do not have to face it. The annoying auntie, the jealous cousin, the bitter sibling, they all make it easier to pull back from family engagements. Even though there are unresolved issues within the family, it would always be better to see your face in the place.

It is possible that your issues run deeper. A mere possibility is that you have kissed one too many frogs and you have vowed to never date again. Sounds extreme, but it happens. Consequently, you have decided it would be best to stay inside and never gather with anyone for the next few years. Your reasons may run the gamut of logical and illogical. Still, it is critical to understand the significance of human interaction. *Two people are better off than one, for they can help each other succeed* (Ecclesiastes 4:9).

Your roof and siding may be damaged if your belief system includes succeeding by yourself. Did I hear you say something? I thought I heard you say it is possible. Well, it depends on your definition of success. Most think of success in terms of material possessions and career status. In spite of that, success involves other components of one's life and should entail your entire being.

Let me be clear. Earlier we discussed vision boarding. Similarly, a few years ago, I created what I call a Vision Book. My Vision Book visually details personal dreams and goals and vision for the future. In the book I define several terms, one of which is success. Here is my distinctive definition: <u>when one is fully aware of their purpose and walking in it</u>. <u>When mind, body, and spirit are healed by speaking it into existence and sharing the journey with others.</u> Any definition of success will involve others in some way.

Healthy partnerships and friendships add value to your life. It is okay to ease into all types of "ships," partnerships, friendships, and romantic relationships. An African Proverb expresses "If you want to go fast, go alone. If you want to go far, go together." This can also happen...

❖You can block your blessing

To block, in any sense of the term, is to stop something from happening. In sports, balls and teammates are blocked. Whether it is a football field or a basketball court, blocking is a part of the game. Yup, it is also a part of the game of life. During hurricane season, residents and business owners use wood to block their windows and doors, which prevents damage to their homes and businesses. It also stops any debris or damaging objects from entering. Seems to be a good thing. Yes, it is. Yet if someone becomes trapped in one of those buildings or homes during a hurricane, this will also block a potential rescuer. Additionally, the wood may reduce the sound coming out of the house. Thereby reducing the chance that someone will hear cries for help.

Here is what I'm getting at. Sometimes when we attempt to block the bad, we can also block the good. It is a risk, I know. But no risk, no reward. I understand there is a fear of being let down again. I acknowledge you have reached the maximum amount of "no's" one can tolerate. I recognize the lies you have been told. But you must continue to believe that your blessing is out there.

Which path will you choose?

What happens if weariness, frustration, or limited thinking sets in and you quit? You will never know what could have been. It is wise to put the wood up *after* leaving the house. Then be sure to remove every inch of it before entering again to keep from getting trapped inside. *Inside* can be interpreted as self-defeating thoughts, wavering emotions, or a dysfunctional past. If you free yourself, you do not need to be rescued. Your roof and siding damage may be able to be repaired if you replace your negative attitude with positive energy and thoughts. Thoughts become actions, which can lead anyone down a different path. Which path will you choose?

In the previous bullet point, we discussed my vision book. This tool can be useful in deciding your path. It is advantageous to write down what you are seeking. Not only are you making the vision plain, but it's also fun to create! Even if your dreams seem lofty, begin to put them in motion. Your vision book or vision board can be as simple or as elaborate as time allows. Make it your own. When you change your thinking, you change your reality. On top of putting your vision on paper, be sure to set daily goals. Some say an idle mind is the devil's playground. There may be some truth to this. An idle mind can become home base for wandering thoughts, guilt, confusion, and temptation. Whether or not you agree, remaining purposeful is key.

In my moments of loneliness, remaining idle was to my detriment. When I chose to simply sit idle without a plan for the day, my thoughts became torturous. The torture came in the form of replaying thoughts of past bad decisions, uncertainty about my future, and unnecessary worry. As human beings with a pulse, some level of worry is inevitable. Parents worry about their children, children worry about their parents, and husbands worry about their wives. But when does it become a burden? Although this is a question you must answer for yourself, the Bible helps us out a bit by giving specific instructions. In fact, it is mentioned many times, which indicates its importance. The two scriptures I would like to reference are: *Can any one of you by worrying add a single hour to your life* (Matthew 6:27)? *And therefore, do not worry about tomorrow, for tomorrow will worry about itself. Each day has enough trouble of its own* (Matthew 6:34). I invite you to take it one day at a time my friend. Remain fully present. Then and only then will you be on the path to "being okay."

SHELTER B

Have you ever murmured the words, "I'll be okay?" No matter the answer, explain your reasoning.

DR. T BOB

What is your storm? What is the root cause of your storm?

Extensive

*"Devastating damage will occur.
Well-built homes, apartment complexes, and industrial
buildings can experience significant damage. Uprooted trees can
block roads and cause property damage."*

Are you constructed well?

Category 3

THE IN-BETWEEN TIME

During your time of aloneness, the in-between time can be a very difficult stage to say the least. If you are thriving through aloneness, you have created a plan and working your faith, believing that at any moment your situation can change. Even so, you may still get a bit weary, wondering how long your plan will take to manifest. The in-between time can seem like forever. This is where it appears that time is at a standstill and nothing is moving or changing. Steps have been taken to change your situation. Still, the walls remain white, the phone remains silent, and your heart is either growing colder or a bit more vulnerable.

If you are not thriving through the in-between time, extensive damage to your construction can occur. Well-built homes, apartment complexes, and industrial buildings can experience significant damage (Categories of Hurricanes |NCHH, 2023). During a Category 3 hurricane, this extensive damage can occur even if buildings are well constructed. It's time to check your nails and screws. Are you put together well? Even if you are built Ford tough, you will always encounter a storm. And because you have identified your storm in the Shelter B activity, your personal storm is now connected to the root problem.

In the case of this Category of a hurricane, the roads will be blocked by falling trees and poles. During the in-between stage, there is also something else that can fall. Silence can fall upon you like the dreariness after a hurricane has passed. It may seem like the worst is behind you. Except it is only the beginning. For the most part, we typically welcome silence as a peaceful break from reality. This is good because we all need quiet moments to relax and think. But in this case, it can be deafening, especially during your time of aloneness. This is a haunting silence that rekindles feelings of singleness, loss, detachment, anxiety, insecurity, and so much more. It introduces you to you.

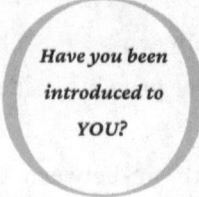

Have you been introduced to you yet? How about intentionally sitting in silence to become one with yourself, to meditate and/or simply receive direction? Most people never sit in silence because they do not like themselves. They do not want to face their reality. It is not easy to face yourself. So what do we do? We escape ourselves by staying busy, focusing on others, and creating excuses for our faults. Because silence is so powerful, I believe each person should begin their day intentionally. The way you begin your day sets the mood for the remainder of the day. I choose to begin each day with a prayer of thanks and declaration, followed by an inspirational reading. Sometimes I will throw in a short sermon by one of my favorite orators.

How will you endure your personal wait time?

As we all know, life is full of surprises. We never know what we may encounter during any given day. Although we cannot fully prepare for many of the things that may come our way, we can try our best. And our best includes knowing exactly who we are and whose we are. So go ahead and turn that deafening silence around to a stillness that demands positive attention; a state of being that helps you understand more about yourself and how to get the most out of each day.

During the in-between phase is where we find our biggest hurdle, WAITING. If you are anything like me, you do not like waiting in long lines at the grocery store, waiting at an extended red light, being placed on hold by customer service representatives, or any waiting for that matter. Nevertheless, waiting is merely something we cannot avoid. While waiting in line at the grocery store, one of the most agitating things is to notice the cashier moving slowly or having to stop to call a supervisor because there is some type of issue. Even though I will eventually get to the register, my anxiety level continues to rise because it seems as if the line will never move. Therefore, I must make the decision to either wait patiently, change lines, or leave. How will you endure your personal wait time?

When waiting for a hurricane to pass through town, we have already received word on what's to come. The sky dims, the rain begins to pour, and the wind quickens. This is not a surprise because it is no different from what you were expecting. However, when you are in the midst of personal waiting, there may not be any indication of what's to come. Impatience and irritation are assured.

Throughout your wait time, wondering if your situation will ever change is quite common. These questions may come to mind: Will you ever find love? Will you ever have kids? Will your kids return home to care for you? Will you achieve your dreams? Will you live a "normal" life again? Believe it or not, these questions are not out of the ordinary. You are not the only one who wonders about such things. Life can be uncertain, and while alone, more time to think can enable a mindset shift.

As I ponder the process of waiting, it reminds me of weather changes. Most can attest to the fact that the weather usually contributes to one's mood. As a Los Angeles, California transplant of 10 years, the City of Angels is certainly known for its sunny days. When the sun illuminates the ocean, it calls for a fun beach day. On a day like this, all beaches are pretty much packed to capacity and residents seem to be filled with joy. Although rainfall is less common in L.A., when it occurs, Californians usually choose to stay in and cuddle up with a good book or movie. On this type of day, it invites a more relaxing feeling. Apart from the sunny weather L.A. is eminent for, the city also experiences its fair share of earthquakes, mudslides, and windstorms. When mother nature rears her ugly head, this can invite an elevated level of anxiety. Just as the weather shifts, our mood shifts. While we wait, there will be continuous repositioning. How will you position yourself on the sunny days, the rainy days, and amidst the catastrophes?

The rate of loneliness in the United States is increasing. Other nations — including Germany, Australia, and the United Kingdom — say that they are facing a loneliness epidemic (Medical News Today, 2020). Didn't I tell you? You may be living through aloneness, but many others are as well. The term "epidemic" seems to be a strong descriptor of loneliness, as compared to other epidemics, such as the Ebola Virus. The average Ebola Virus case fatality rate is around 50%. Case fatality rates have varied from 25% to 90% in past outbreaks (World Health Organization, 2021). This may lead some to wonder why loneliness would also be labeled an epidemic. Seems as though there is no comparison. Or is there?

Though the waiting period may sometimes seem tumultuous, there are what I call powerful side effects of waiting. One side effect is *endurance*. Another is *flexibility*. Now there are some parts of us that may suffer during the in-between time. In mental health, there are associations between loneliness and depression, anxiety, phobias, suicide/parasuicide, dementia, eating disorders and psychosis (Psych Scene Hub, 2020). Contemporary psychiatry has also incorporated loneliness on two diagnostic levels: a personality trait and a clinical symptom (Psychiatric Times, 2020).

> Can the side effects of your loneliness be fatal?

So, is loneliness an epidemic? Can lonely people suffer fatal injuries? I absolutely believe so. Let's discuss how this can happen. If there isn't any intentional differentiation between being alone and being lonely, unfortunately, you are already off to an unhealthy start. As we have discovered, loneliness is a thing.

The side effects can make or break you. And sometimes both may happen simultaneously. If you allow yourself to dwell in anxiety, this can lead to depression, which can lead to bad decisions, which can also affect your physical health. And worst of all, the feelings of sadness may become so unbearable, you choose not to live through it and ultimately end your life. This is why I encourage you to embrace the side effects of *endurance* and *flexibility*. And while you're at it, coat those with *tenacity* and *patience*. To embrace the positive concept of aloneness is essential.

Though the feelings of loneliness remain, doing so will prevent you from getting caught up in the eyewall of the storm. The eyewall may develop in the form of mental illness. General knowledge of mental illness via family situations, social media, schools, or even television is standard. I'd like to help expand on pre-existing knowledge by explaining the basics of some of the mental health disorders associated with loneliness. In my clinical experience, loneliness may lead to psychiatric disorders and diseases, including but not limited to Depression, Alcoholism and Alzheimer's Disease. Depression, otherwise known as major depressive disorder or clinical depression, is a common and serious mood disorder. Those who suffer from depression experience persistent feelings of sadness and hopelessness and lose interest in activities they once enjoyed. Aside from the emotional problems caused by depression, individuals can also present with physical symptoms such as chronic pain or digestive issues. To be diagnosed with depression, symptoms must be present for at least two weeks (The Diagnostic and Statistical Manual of Mental Disorders, 5th Edition).

Alcohol Use Disorder is a problematic pattern of alcohol use leading to clinically significant impairment or distress, as manifested by at least two of specific criteria, occurring within a 12-month period. Any of this sound familiar yet? Well, Alzheimer's Disease is a diagnosis assigned to individuals who are experiencing cognitive deficits directly related to the onset and progression of Alzheimer's Dementia. Alzheimer's Dementia is a neurological disorder in which an individual experiences progressive cognitive dysfunction due to the incursion of beta-amyloid plaques and neurofibrillary tangles in cholinergic neurons. The acetylcholine production of the affected neurons decreases, which is clinically manifested as progressive memory loss, and associated behavioral symptoms (DSM-5).

Deep, right? I know. Let's get into it a little more. There are also Personality Disorders associated with loneliness, including Borderline and Schizoid Disorder. The Borderline pattern qualifier may be applied to individuals whose pattern of personality disturbance is characterized by a pervasive pattern of instability and interpersonal relationships, self-image, and affects, and marked impulsivity, as indicated by 5 or more specific criteria (DSM-5).

Schizoid Personality Disorder is a pervasive pattern of social and interpersonal deficits marked by acute discomfort with, and reduced capacity to form close relationships, as well as by cognitive or perceptual distortions and eccentricities of behavior, beginning by early adulthood and present in a variety of contexts (DSM-5).

All the above can happen in-between time, in between behaving as if all is well, in between choosing loneliness and not aloneness, in between pretending you are "okay," and ultimately in between choosing not to answer yourself by challenging negative thoughts. What does your in-between time look like?

SHELTER C

List 3 positive actionable steps you can take while WAITING for your breakthrough.

DR. T BOB

What poor behaviors have you participated in during your in-between time?

Extreme

*"Catastrophic damage will occur.
Well-built buildings can see intense structural damage and
make areas uninhabitable due to a lack of power.
Significant risk of physical harm."*

Is your building uninhabitable?

Category 4

GHOSTS OF THE PAST

Take a moment to think of your earliest memory. Get into a comfortable position and take yourself back to that moment. Five.... Four....Three....Two....One—what's the memory? What type of feelings come up for you? Did this moment bring happy, sad, exciting, or disturbing feelings back to your body? I invite you to rest there for a moment.

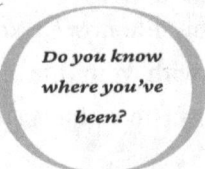

Do you know where you've been?

This may or may not be a comfortable memory. Still, whatever emotion is happening right now, embrace it. It is very important to recall past events. Many times we avoid memories that bring pain along with them. We can sometimes unknowingly repress those memories because they hurt too much. Ever talk to someone about a painful factual event they experienced and they deny it ever occurred? Yes, they may be guilty of telling a tale. Nonetheless, it can also be a form of repression. Sigmund Freud, known as the father of psychoanalysis, and daughter Anna Freud, clearly defined the term *defense mechanisms*. *Repression* is a defense mechanism that may be present in someone who has no recollection of a traumatic event, even though they were conscious and aware during the event. In the twentieth century, she defined repression as subconsciously blocking ideas or impulses that are undesirable (National Library of Medicine, 2022).

So therein lies the question, are you repressing any painful memories? The best way to answer this question is to meet with a Mental Health Professional. A trained professional can help you to recover these thoughts and guide you through the process of healing. To know where you're going, you must know where you've been. When working with clients, I always like to delve into their childhood. We must explore early life before we move into the future. Those who have experienced a troubled childhood may say things like "I've moved on from that" or "what does that have to do with my life now?" Well it pretty much has everything to do with your life now. Many early experiences have the power to influence our adult decisions and behaviors.

It's a possibility your father left at an early age and ever since, abandonment issues have been prevalent. Or early abuse occurred, and in adulthood, continuing to choose those who treat you negatively, or displaying abusive behavior to others is a characteristic. Your parents may enjoy a healthy long-lasting marriage and you believe your mate will model those identical characteristics of your loving parents. I could go on and on. But I think you get it. You're a smart bunch.

There is much to unpack as it relates to the connectivity of early and current life. For that reason, treat personal memories with care. They are a part of your makeup. Without them, you would not be who you are. And without healing, those memories will continue to have a negative effect on your present and future, whether you admit it or not. Here is where we make the mistake of answering ourselves by denying facts. Be sure to use the technique of answering yourself to remain truthful and empowered. Even if you think you are too old to work through some of those memories, do it anyway. Age doesn't matter here. Yes, you have made it this far. But imagine how much better your quality of life would be as an emotionally whole person. Ask yourself:

→ How do I treat others?
→ Do I believe most people are verbally attacking me?
→ Do I shy away from uncomfortable topics?
→ Do I express my emotions well?
→ Am I affectionate? Why or why not?
→ Am I okay with discussing my past?
→ Do I have difficulty making friends?
→ Do I have difficulty maintaining romantic and familial relationships?
→ Am I short-tempered?
→ Does my mood shift quickly?

→ Do I struggle with forgiveness?

Now reflect on your answers. Your responses may be an indication of poor or optimal mental and emotional health. What areas need improvement? As human beings walking the earth, we all have areas that need improvement, but it is about becoming whole. Yeah, there's that *whole* word I mentioned earlier. When thinking of the descriptor *whole—full, complete,* and *lacking nothing* comes to mind.

Wholeness can be tied to waiting, and it doesn't happen overnight. It includes accepting the process of healing. To achieve wholeness, there will be trials and tribulations if you will. Still and all, this is the process. James 2: 1-4 says *Count it all joy when you fall into various trials, knowing that the testing of your faith produces patience. But let patience have its perfect work, that you may be perfect and complete, lacking nothing.*

Although there may be some separation among people in your life, it's best to simply work through other issues in your journey to completeness. Why? Because every issue cannot simply be thrown away. I'm reminded of the decision made to improve my diet, and I thought a blender might help with my smoothie efforts. It was said that it would be best to purchase a blender that extracts, or better yet, a juicer. At the time, I did not fully understand the recommendation, thinking all blenders pretty much did the same thing. However, I learned that in the extraction process, the extractor breaks through the tough stuff to access the hidden nutrition. Nothing is thrown away. Did you catch that? Becoming whole includes breaking through the tough stuff, not ignoring it or behaving as if it did not happen. The continuous journey of healing brings you to wholeness. It does not indicate perfection. In fact, it embraces your flaws and confirms your journey of purpose and imperfection. To be whole is to be complete, mind-body-spirit.

Because this level of loneliness can potentially cause catastrophic damage, one must be very careful. Here is where those intimidating and guilt-ridden voices come into play again. The vivid movie of those failed relationships, or that one thing, two or ten things you've done that no one else knows about begins to play in your head. Day by day, those visions and thoughts start to eat away at you slowly. Thought after thought, they gradually steal your joy. Although some do not recognize when practicing such behavior, living in the past is quite an unhealthy habit. This concept may be a bit difficult to process. So let me offer a bit of clarity.

Earlier we spoke of resolving past issues by confronting them and seeking professional help. Again, this is healthy. On the contrary, when one constantly reminds themselves of past behaviors, allows guilt to monopolize their emotions, and moves according to what they have experienced in the past, they may in fact stunt their emotional growth. There is a normal developmental process, as well as an abnormal development process. An example of abnormal development may include those who experience traumatic events at an early age. This may halt their emotional or mental development.

Who are you? I opened this chapter by asking you to take yourself back to your earliest memory, whether good or bad. This was done to help you realize who you are - all of you. Sometimes we forget who we are and need to be reminded. Let's remember, during the Category 4 stage of a hurricane, buildings are wrecked and affected areas may be uninhabitable for days or weeks (Categories of Hurricanes |NCHH, 2023). Uninhabitable implies there is no safe or healthy space to occupy. Is your mind uninhabitable? Is your physical body uninhabitable? Are you simply a shell of a human walking the earth? Have you caused so much damage that your building is wrecked? No matter what has happened to you or what you have put yourself through, you must allow positive thoughts to inhabit your mind and sensible behaviors to inhabit your body.

Do you mind if we dive into "structural damage" just for a moment? Okay, let's do it! We have covered more than enough ways to bring damage to your temple. But there is one way you may not have considered. It is the demon of unforgiveness. One must have a specific stance and be able to outline specific reasons as to why their decision of unforgiveness is valid. Forgiveness is particularly difficult when someone has wronged you and caused you some level of pain. The level of pain can determine your willingness to forgive. I am not an expert on forgiveness. But here is what I know: it begins the process of healing, it eliminates the emotional weight, it frees your mind, and ultimately, the benefit is yours, not the person who has wronged you. If unforgiveness is held in your body, building wreckage will continually happen. Let's see what the manual for life says on the topic of forgiveness. *Therefore, as the elect of God, holy and beloved, put-on tender mercies, kindness, humility, meekness, longsuffering; bearing with one another, and forgiving one another, if anyone has a complaint against another; even as Christ forgave you, so you also must do.* (Colossians 3:12-13). The key to forgiving others is remembering how much God has forgiven you.

Now I am sure you've figured out by now that your "building" can be equated to your physical "body." I will utilize the word *temple* interchangeably with *body*. You were blessed with a temple at birth. As we progress through life, we choose to either care for our temple or neglect it. Or if you're anything like me, your choice probably fluctuates depending on the season. Oftentimes, when most think of treating their body well, they think of working out and eating healthy. These are certainly great ways to take good care of your temple. A healthy diet and a consistent workout plan are usually recipes for good health. Hmmm, but what about your "audio and visual diet"?

Never heard of those types of diets? I know, just made them up. Our "audio diet" is what we listen to and what we tell ourselves and others. Our "visual diet" is what we watch and witness. Both must be monitored carefully. There are certain songs, television content, or social media posts that may trigger past or current turmoil. Once we are triggered, this may lead to unfavorable thoughts, which can then lead to regrettable behavior. Oh, here is one more—our "people diet!" There are just certain people we should not share space with. You know exactly who they are. But just in case you need help, here's a hint. Those people who discourage instead of encourage. Those people who refuse to grow and would like you to do the same. Those people who consistently cause your stress level to increase. And those people you continually pour into, still their emptiness prevails. Try embracing a full diet. Your temple will be thankful.

As we see, being healthy, whole, and taking care of your building is not just about showing up physically fit, it is about being okay with YOU. This leads us to the most important practice of releasing yourself from "Ghosts of the Pasts." Here goes...forgiving YOURSELF. Yep, this is the big one. Forgiving others is only the first step. The next step of forgiving yourself can be a doozy.

Do you recall my utilization of the term *imperfect* over the course of this book? Hopefully, you answered "yes." Therefore, my confidence lies in your knowledge of personal imperfections. This is vital when going through the stages of self-forgiveness. There are past behaviors you may have difficulty forgiving yourself for. They typically run the gamut; such as, you know you could have handled that situation differently. You know you should not have given in to peer pressure. You know you should have followed your gut feeling. You know you should have paid attention to those red flags. You know you should have left when you had the chance. You know you should have resisted temptation. You know you could have been more patient. You know you could have spoken up.

For some, those unhealthy choices were made over a decade ago. Continuing to press play and attempting to edit the result will not expedite the process of self-forgiveness. In other circumstances, there was not anything that could have been done on your behalf to change the outcome of the situation. Here is what is important to understand: you made the best decision with the knowledge possessed at the time. You must do the best with the knowledge you have until you learn more. When you know more, use that knowledge to make better decisions. Other instances include being vulnerable due to previous circumstances and/or simply not being in a healthy space. Not forgiving yourself is a sure way to bring extreme damage to your building. It is the epitome of a Category 4 hurricane.

Our temple is the most important thing we possess. It includes our heart and soul. *I beseech you therefore, brethren, by the mercies of God, that you present your bodies a living sacrifice, holy, acceptable to God, which is your reasonable service* (Romans 12:1). Life is short; for that reason, time is of the essence. So I invite you to forgive yourself. It will change the quality of your life.

SHELTER D

From a minor offense to a major offense, who do you need to forgive and why?

DR. T BOB

What do you need to forgive yourself for? What do you believe you will gain by forgiving yourself?

Catastrophic

*"Catastrophic damage will occur.
A storm this intense can cause total roof damage, blow out windows, and flatten some older homes. Homes in the community may be without power and drinkable water for months."*

What's your recovery time?

Category 5

SELF-MEDICATING PRESCRIPTIVE ACTIVITIES

Will your structure outlast this storm? Here is where you come to a crossroad of sorts. Which direction will you choose? Instead of indulging in defeatist behaviors to ignore the obvious threat of destruction, it is wise to involve yourself in productive practices. Amid finding strength to elevate from loneliness to aloneness, one must be intentional. Your intentional behavior will influence your recovery time.

Recovery time is the space allowed to get to a healthy place where you are comfortable and fulfilled in your own skin, whether you are alone or surrounded by loving people. You can choose to endure your recovery time by popping pills, abusing alcohol, overspending, sleeping around, consuming illicit drugs, or flat out making bad choices. *Or*, you can choose to complete my prescription of self-medicating activities. They can cover you when the storm begins to rage.

PRESCRIPTION #1

Create a weekly to-do list. Be sure to make it neat and
colorful. Each time you complete a task,
draw a line through it or check it off.

DR. T BOB

PRESCRIPTION #2

Be honest. Have you ever compared yourself to anyone? Think thoroughly about this. If so, list their names here.

It's Okay To Answer Yourself

What was the comparison?

Do you believe there are possibly things you do not know about this person (relationship, personal, career, etc.)?

It's Okay To Answer Yourself

List a few assumptions about their situation that may be less than ideal.

DR. T BOB

PRESCRIPTION #3

At a minimum, check in with yourself once per week. Choose a day of the week to ask, "How am I?" Be honest with yourself and specific with your response.

It's Okay To Answer Yourself

PRESCRIPTION #4

Document your "visual diet."
List five television shows you are watching.

DR. T BOB

List positive messages you have received from the shows.

It's Okay To Answer Yourself

List negative messages you have received from the shows.

DR. T BOB

Are there any shows you should eliminate? If so, list here.

It's Okay To Answer Yourself

PRESCRIPTION #5

Document your "audio diet."
List podcasts, albums, and/or books you enjoy listening to.

DR. T BOB

List positive messages you have received from the content/lyrics.

It's Okay To Answer Yourself

List negative messages you have received from the content/lyrics.

DR. T BOB

Is there any content you should eliminate? If so, list here.

It's Okay To Answer Yourself

PRESCRIPTION #6

Document your "people diet." List three humans you consistently communicate or hang out with.

DR. T BOB

List three positive characteristics of each person.

It's Okay To Answer Yourself

List characteristics of each person that may possibly distract you from moving in your purpose.

DR. T BOB

Should you minimize your time with any of them? If so, list their names here. *Be sure to stand firm on this.*

It's Okay To Answer Yourself

PRESCRIPTION #7

The next time you have a self-defeating thought,
write the thought here:

DR. T BOB

Now write a positive thought to combat the above thought.
What's your "answer" to yourself?

It's Okay To Answer Yourself

Take a moment to reflect and write out your thoughts below:

DR. T BOB

PRESCRIPTION #8

Close your eyes and think of the word "love."
List adjectives that immediately come to mind.

It's Okay To Answer Yourself

Now write your personal definition of love.

What does your personal definition of love look like in real life? Give a descriptive example.

PRESCRIPTION #9

Do you have "unfinished business" with someone? Do you seek closure about an unresolved situation? Choose one of the options below to complete. Or if you're feeling emotionally healthy, do both!

> A. Place two chairs in the center of the room. Sit in one chair and imagine the person you have unfinished business with is in the other chair. Verbalize everything you have ever wanted to say to this person. No holds barred. You can yell, swear, cry, fight, or whisper. But at the end of the conversation, be sure to make amends and get the closure you need.

> B. Write a letter to the person with whom you seek closure. In this letter, be sure to express all your feelings. Do not leave anything out. Take the time you need. This may require writing the letter over several days. At the end of the letter, be sure to make amends and get the closure you need to move on. You can choose to mail the letter or simply place it in your journal for later reflection.

PRESCRIPTION #10

Create an affirmation list specifically targeted to your areas of struggle. To **affirm** is to state as a fact or assert strongly or publicly. **Affirmation** is the action or process of affirming something or being affirmed.

Please begin each statement with "I." Speak aloud daily.

I AM WORTHY!

* _____
* _____
* _____
* _____
* _____
* _____
* _____
* _____
* _____
* _____
* _____
* _____
* _____
* _____
* _____

Notes

DR. T BOB

It's Okay To Answer Yourself

DR. T BOB

It's Okay To Answer Yourself

DR. T BOB

It's Okay To Answer Yourself

DR. T BOB

It's Okay To Answer Yourself

Epilogue

While discussing a previous courtship with a family member, she asked "Don't you get lonely?" My response was "Of course I do. But I'm not going to lay with just anyone to avoid the feeling." Many times we find ourselves filling space with a warm body as a temporary fix; all while knowing it's a bad idea. Temporary highs only make us feel lower when we come down. If the "stuff" going on inside of you during your time of aloneness is not acknowledged, the results can be life-threatening in more ways than one.

For me, loneliness came at different times. To my benefit, these are the times I was most productive. Ultimately, making a choice about how to utilize the circumstance set before me was key. Because life goes on during these times, one may experience further loss in the form of friendships, death, jobs, etc. This can be particularly difficult when there is no support system present.

During my time of aloneness, I experienced broken friendships, broken family relationships, death, deceit, unemployment, confusion, and doubt about my existence. Therefore, I get it!

As a little girl, going outside was not much fun for me. Playing alone with my dolls was much more enjoyable. As maturation occurred, I was introduced to the term <u>introvert</u>, which generally describes those who feel more comfortable focusing on their inner thoughts and ideas, rather than what's happening externally. They enjoy spending time with just one or two people rather than in large groups or crowds (Ellis, 2022). There you have it! I thought "This is totally me." Although many believe I display extroverted characteristics, introvertedness is my jam. If this sounds familiar to you, take time and research introverts vs. extroverts. Now if you find that you are an introvert, it still does not validate your decision to unwillingly spend time with others. Although introverts need a certain amount of time alone, you were created to coexist with other humans. Nah, I'm not fully feeling this either, because people are flat out weird at times. But so are you! You did not know that about yourself, huh? I know; it's hard to see ourselves.

Feelings of loneliness will come and go just as night and day does. The good news is the sun will always shine again. After a short time of experiencing the shallow feeling of loneliness, I decided to thrive through aloneness. Once you discover your reason for being on earth, understanding that nothing should and can stop

It's Okay To Answer Yourself

your momentum comes naturally. Distractions can temporarily set you back, but shall not stop you. With the strongest weapon being the infiltration of your thoughts, it will do everything in its power to do so.

As we all have fallen short, please know you can always get back up again. There is no rule that says you cannot start over. So dust yourself off and begin again. Amidst it all, be sure to answer yourself with the most **sensible**, **positive**, **uplifting**, and **motivating** responses you can muster up. And when responding, above all, **believe in yourself**. If you don't, no one else will.

I'll leave you with this. In those moments when you feel there is no strength to go on, take a step anyway. There were times I've been so fatigued, rest was not only needed, but required. We all need healthy breaks from time to time. It will give us time to recharge and reconnect. *Come to me, all you who are weary and burdened, and I will give you rest. Take my yoke upon you and learn from me, for I am gentle and humble in heart, and you will find rest for your souls. For my yoke is easy and my burden is light* (Matthew 11:28-30). Allow Jesus to embrace you. Be comforted my friend.

Bibliography

2021. "Ebola virus disease." World Health Organization.

2023. "Deoxyribonucleic Acid (DNA)." National Human Genome Research Institute.

2023. "Extremely Powerful Hurricane Katrina Leaves a Historic Mark on the Northern Gulf Coast." National Weather Service.

Adams, Z. 2021. "How can we minimize Instagram's harmful effects?" American Psychological Association.

Alarcon, R.D. 2020. "Mental Health in a Pandemic State: The Route From Social Isolation to Loneliness." Psychiatric Times.

American Psychiatric Association. Diagnostic and Statistical Manual of Mental Disorders, 5th Edition.

"Categories of Hurricanes |NCHH." National Center for Healthy Housing, June 2023.

Ellis, R.R. 2022 "Introvert Personality." Web MD

Leonard, J. 2020. "What are the effects of solitary confinement on health?" Medical News Today.

Life Application Study Bible.

Mann, F. 2020. "Loneliness and Mental Health Problems in Adults: Isolating the Evidence." Psych scene hub.

Various authors. 2018. "Stress effects on the body." American Psychological Association.

Zukor, T. 2020. "Balancing anxiety - negative vs. positive COVID-19 thinking." Journal of Counseling Psychology.

About the Author

As she rode the waves through her personal storm of failed relationships and singleness, Dr. T-Bob gained a particular interest in sharing her wisdom with those who struggle to find shelter through such a season. A lifelong resident of New Orleans, Louisiana, Dr. T-Bob earned a Doctor of Philosophy and Master of Education in the discipline of Counseling from the University of New Orleans and Southeastern Louisiana University, along with a Bachelor of Science in Psychology from Northwestern State University. Dr. T-Bob's Christian upbringing, merged with her experience in academia and motivational speaking, contributes to her success as a faith-based Counselor Educator. On any given starry night, you may find her performing on stages around the world or penning the next big Hollywood Blockbuster film.

www.ingramcontent.com/pod-product-compliance
Lightning Source LLC
LaVergne TN
LVHW030311070526
838199LV00007B/371